Endangered Mammals

Julie Haydon

Contents

Rigby.

Endangered Mammals

Mammals are **warm-blooded** animals that often have fur or hair. They give birth to live young. They make milk for their young.

A panda with its young

Endangered mammals are in danger of becoming **extinct**. Some mammals become extinct **naturally**. But some mammals are endangered today because of people.

A black rhinoceros with its young

A land clearing

A conservation worker

Sometimes people:
- Destroy a mammal's **habitat** when they clear land or pollute the land and water
- **Capture** or kill wild mammals

Conservation efforts are helping save some endangered mammals from becoming extinct.

Northern Hairy-nosed Wombat

Scientific name:
Lasiorhinus krefftii
(say *lazy-o-rhi-nus kref-tee-ee*)

Status:
critically endangered

Lives:
Queensland,
Australia

Queensland

Australia

Description

The northern hairy-nosed wombat has a large, solid body with big ears and a short tail. It has brownish-gray fur. It lives in burrows and comes out at night to feed on grass.

It is endangered because:
- Its habitat is being destroyed
- It is killed by foxes and **feral** cats
- It has to compete for food with cattle, sheep, and rabbits

ENDANGERED

A feral cat

Conservation efforts

The northern hairy-nosed wombat is **protected**. The only known group, or **colony**, lives in a national park in Queensland. It is hoped the colony's numbers will increase.

ENDA...
Snow
Leopard

Scientific name:
Uncia uncia
(say *un-key-a un-key-a*)

Status:
endangered

Lives:
mountains in parts
of central Asia

Mongolia

China

Nepal Bhutan

India

Pakistan

Description

The snow leopard has a thick, gray coat with black spots. It lives in mountains and **alpine** forests and hunts wild goats and sheep.

It is endangered because:
• It is hunted for its fur

A snow leopard's pelt

- It is killed for its bones, which are used in **traditional** medicines
- There are fewer wild goats and sheep for it to hunt
- It is killed by farmers protecting their livestock

Conservation efforts

National parks in parts of central Asia have been set up to protect the snow leopard.

Giant Panda

Description

The giant panda is a large, bear-like mammal with a thick, black and white coat. It is shy and usually lives alone. The giant panda's main diet is a woody plant called bamboo.

It is endangered because:
- It is killed for its fur
- Its habitat is being destroyed

Conservation efforts

The giant panda is protected and many live in **reserves**. Its future is looking brighter.

Scientific name:
Ailuropoda melanoleuca
(say *eil-u-ro-po-da me-lan-o-lew-ka*)

Status:
endangered

Lives:
mountains in China

Mongolia

China

India

The giant panda feeds on bamboo plants.

Volcano Rabbit

Scientific name:
Romerolagus diazi
(say *rome-e-ro-lag-us die-arzi*)

Status:
endangered

Lives:
Mexico

United States

Mexico

Description

The volcano rabbit is one of the world's smallest rabbits. It lives in forests on the sides of volcanoes in Mexico. It feeds on grasses found in the forests.

Cattle grazing

Conservation efforts

People are trying to protect the volcano rabbit by replanting trees and grasses in the forests where it lives. The volcano rabbit is also being bred in zoos. These animals may one day be released into the wild.

It is endangered because:
- It is killed for food
- Its habitat is being destroyed
- It now has to compete for food with grazing animals

ENDANGER

Arabian oryx,
Middle East

Giant panda, China

Orangutan, Borneo and Su

12   Black rhinoceros, Africa

Snow leopard, Central Asia

Red wolf,
Eastern United States

Volcano rabbit, Mexico

Northern hairy-nosed wombat,
Australia

13

Orangutan

Scientific name:
Pongo pygmaeus
(say *pong-go
pig-may-us*)

Status:
endangered

Lives:
islands of Sumatra
and Borneo

South China Sea

Borneo

Sumatra

Description

The orangutan is an ape. It has reddish-brown fur and long arms. It spends most of its time in trees in rain forests. It eats fruit, leaves, insects, and small animals.

It is endangered because:

- Its habitat is being destroyed
- It is killed out of fear, for food, and for sport
- It is captured for the **live animal trade**

Conservation efforts

The orangutan is protected, and many live in reserves and national parks. Some orangutans that were **illegally** captured and kept as pets have been returned to the wild.

The orangutan's habitat is being destroyed.

ENDANGERED

Red Wolf

Scientific name:
Canis rufus
(say *ca-nis roo-fuss*)

Status:
critically endangered

Lives:
eastern United States

United States

Description

The red wolf looks like a dog. It has reddish-brown fur and big ears. It lives in packs and hunts small mammals.

It is endangered because:

- It was killed out of fear and for sport
- Its habitat is being destroyed
- It mates with **coyotes**, so there are fewer pure red wolves

ENDANGERED

A coyote

Conservation efforts

The red wolf was extinct in the wild by 1980. It only survived because red wolves in zoos were bred and **reintroduced** to the wild. There are plans for more red wolves born in zoos to be returned to the wild.

Black Rhinoceros

Scientific name:
Diceros bicornis
(say *di-ke-ross
bye-cor-nis*)

Status:
critically endangered

Lives:
Africa

Africa

Atlantic
Ocean

Description

The black rhinoceros is a huge, solid animal. It eats plants and usually lives alone. It has four short legs and two horns on its snout.

It is endangered because:
- It is killed for its horns, which are used in traditional medicines and in knife handles
- It is killed for its hide, out of fear, and for sport
- Its habitat is being destroyed

Conservation efforts

In some African countries, wildlife officials are sawing the horns off live rhinos to save them from being hunted and killed.

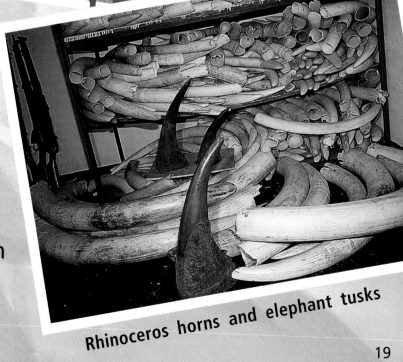

Rhinoceros horns and elephant tusks

Arabian Oryx

Scientific name:
Oryx leucoryx
(say *o-rix lew-ko-rix*)

Status:
endangered

Lives:
Middle East

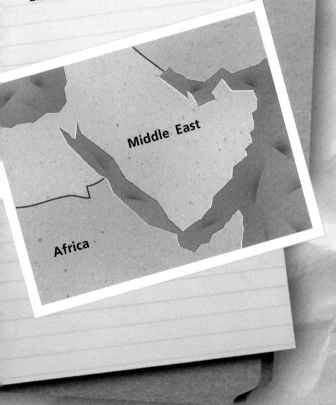

Middle East

Africa

Description

The Arabian oryx is an antelope with long, sharp horns. It lives in herds in deserts and dry plains. It eats plants.

It is endangered because:

- It is killed for food
- It has to compete for food with livestock

Conservation efforts

The Arabian oryx was extinct in the wild by 1972. Small herds were bred in zoos and reintroduced to the wild.

The desert is home to the Arabian oryx.

Saving Endangered Mammals

Many people are trying to save endangered mammals by:
- Saving habitats
- Making laws to protect the mammals
- Making national parks and reserves where the mammals can live safely
- Teaching people about endangered mammals
- Breeding endangered mammals in zoos

This park ranger protects endangered animals.

These rhinoceroses live in a national park.

ENDANGERED

This panda was bred in a zoo.

Glossary

alpine in or near high mountains

capture to catch, to take prisoner

colony a group of animals of the same kind that live together

conservation protection of the environment, including animals and plants

coyotes wild dogs that live in North America

critically very much

extinct died out

feral wild

habitat the area where an animal lives, eats, and breeds

illegally against the law

live animal trade the act of catching and selling wild animals as pets or to zoos, sometimes illegally

naturally to do with nature or caused by nature, not people

protected kept from harm. It is against the law to catch or kill a protected animal.

reintroduced taught how to live in the wild, then set free

reserves areas where animals are protected

traditional relating to long-held customs and beliefs

warm-blooded an animal whose body temperature stays the same and does not rise and fall with the temperature of its surroundings

Index